The Subtle Art of Branding

Compiled and Edited by Alaa Abouelhassan

The Subtle Art Of Branding

Combiled and Edited: Alaa Abouelhassan.

Credit: Susan Friedmann.   *Jonathan Brown*   *Bob Zurn.*   *Rob Sullivan.*   *Tyson Fenech.*   *Ray Smith*

1. Brand Name: The Six Quintessential Factors You Must Know.

Choosing a name for your new business isn't simple. A name accomplishes more than distinguish your organization. It tells clients your identity, what you do, and quite about how you do it. Your name separates you from your companions, crests client premium, and welcomes further examination - on the off chance that you do it right.

I didn't do it right. In any event, not at first.

All business people commit errors, and I made one of my initial ones immediately. Excited with the juvenile business I was beginning, this valuable undertaking so important to me, I initiated my organization Diadem Communications. Diadem implies crown- - a fitting name for what I felt was a crowning achievement.

most distinguished accomplishment.

What does Diadem say to you? Does it inspire musings of me coming into your organization, preparing your business group to be the best stall staff regularly, guaranteeing that each and every public expo you go to ends up being incredibly fruitful? Does it make me sound so great that you just can hardly wait to contract me?

No. It doesn't express that to me either. Furthermore, surprisingly more terrible, it didn't express that to any of my potential clients. Passing by name alone, nobody would almost certainly decide even the slightest bit of data about me, my organization, or the administrations we offer. The name said nothing, and it did nothing for me.

The name needed to go. All the more vitally, it must be supplanted by something compelling. How would you think of a compelling name? Think about these six components:

An Effective Name:

1. **Reveals to Who You Are**: Your name ought to mirror your character. This is a fundamental part of marking. You'll be advancing this name, getting it before however many eyes as could

be expected under the circumstances as frequently as would be prudent. How would you need the general population to consider you?

For a few, that implies coordinating your own name into the name of your business. This is exceptionally normal in certain callings: lawful, medicinal, and bookkeeping jump to mind.

Others incline toward a progressively spellbinding name. One effective little bread cook maintains her business under the name "The Cookie Lady" since that is the means by which her first clients recognized her. It's far fetched that the vast majority of the clients even know her first name (It's

Pat) however everyone in her market knows "The Cookie Lady".

2. **Reveals to What You Do**: It's mind boggling what number of organization names give nearly nothing, if any sign of what kind of work the association really does. Take the accompanying models:

-Smith and Sons.

-Hulbert Brothers.

-Only One.
Would you be able to reveal to me what any of these organizations does? Obviously, you can't. They're depending on clients definitely knowing their identity (a dubious suggestion for new organizations!) or by having their name found in 'setting, for example, a business index or on-line professional reference.

3. **Reveals to How You Do It**: Words are extremely amazing. Via cautiously choosing what words you use in your name, you can pass on a lot about your organization's picture.

Consider the names of three distinctive back rub and bodywork focuses:

-Champlain Valley Therapeutic Massage.

-Clouds Above Massage.

-Speedy Spa.

Each of the three organizations is giving a similar administration: rub treatment. However the first seems to support a progressively medicinal methodology, the second, a fantastic, extravagance approach, and the third spotlights on quick administration.

4. **Separates You From Your Peers**: Your organization name is the principal chance to tell clients how you vary from the challenge. This should be possible by underlining what makes you extraordinary, pinpointing what part of your items and administrations can't be found anyplace else - or that you show improvement over any other individual.

Consider the back rub treatment model we took a gander at in number three. Every association plainly has an alternate concentration and way to deal with their client base. They're pulling in various sorts of customers, who are looking for on a very basic level diverse methodologies. Which is all passed on in under five words.

5. **Pinnacles Customer Interest**: Creating client intrigue is a workmanship and a science. Ponder your intended interest group. What characteristics of your administrations are of the best import to your clients? What sort of words are probably

going to speak to them?

Underline the critical characteristics in your name. For instance, occupied mortgage holders are attracted to the inalienable guarantee of speed offered by "Bounce's Instant Plumbing" while a peruser looking for a decent riddle will incline toward "Wrongdoing Pays Books".

Word decision is likewise vital. Two yarn shops can both work in claim to fame strands, yet the person who marks themselves "Constantly" will attract a quite unexpected group in comparison to the one named "Normal Beauty: Organic Yarns".

6. **Welcomes Further Investigation**: Customers are amusing animals. What one gathering observes to be entertaining and connecting with turns another gathering off. You need

your name to welcome and congenial - as those characteristics are seen by your intended interest group.

The best case of this might be found in the individual speculator fragment of the monetary administrations industry. Charles Schwab has invested years developing a work of art, formal picture - however at this point, the customer base is evolving from 'elderly individuals with

cash' to 'everybody with a 401K', Charles Schwab has propelled the

"Converse with Chuck" crusade with an end goal to be progressively agreeable.

Ensure your name doesn't scare clients away! A few enterprises are more formal than others, however, embrace claim at your hazard.

Subsequent to following a progression of basic well-ordered directions to coordinate my corporate character with my administration offering, I concocted the quintessential name: The Trade Show Coach. This name in a split second tells clients what I do - help organizations with public exhibitions - and a tad bit of the way in which I do it - mentor, as opposed to manage, direct, control, or sort out.

See the distinction? So did the purchasing open, some of who rapidly turned into my best clients. A similar thing can occur for you - on the off chance that you pick the correct name.

2.How to protect Your Corporate Name:

Envision this: you need to sell gadgets, and you've picked the ideal name for your fresh out of the plastic new gadget business. You've made the name unique but comfortable, simple to state, hard to overlook, and you've checked databases wherever to ensure that no one else thought of it first. You've put huge wholes of cash in advertising materials and retail facade signs that incorporate your great new name. The best part is that you've effectively awed some new gadget clients with your stunning administrations and they are getting the message out that your business-indeed, the one with your breathtakingly one of a kind name-is the spot to go for all their gadget needs, without exception. You cherish your new name.

At that point picture this: not long after your gadget shop opens for business, you discover that a person two squares over is utilizing a similar

name, for a strikingly comparative gadget business. That is your name hanging in his window, by God! Clients are getting confounded. Your business starts to drop off and you presume the other gadget fellow is getting the clients who were searching for you.

Is this bad dream situation conceivable?

Tragically, yes-however just on the off chance that you don't have a clue how to ensure your corporate name legitimately.

The principal thing another entrepreneur must do is register the name of the new partnership. The methodology for enlistment fluctuates by state, yet for the most part includes some exceptionally straightforward administrative work to be submitted to the state's Secretary of State's office, alongside a little expense. The Secretary of State's office won't enroll two organizations with a similar name, so this methodology will keep later organizations from consolidating in a similar state under your corporate name. Enlistment with the Secretary of State's office will likewise legitimize the corporate personality of your business as a legitimate element separate from its organizers, and will give proof to show that the name is being utilized in trade when you next register the name as a trademark. Know, in any case, that a business can consolidate in any of the fifty states, so enlisting your business in your own state gives just fractional security of your corporate name. To give more noteworthy assurance, it is important to enroll the name as a trademark or administration mark with the United States Patent and Trademark Office.

Enrolling your new business name with the U.S. Patent and Trademark Office will give across the nation notice of your case to the name as a trademark, and summons the purview of the government courts in securing the name.

To enlist another business name as a trademark, an application might be gotten online at the U.S. Patent and Trademark site, www.uspto.gov. This application may either be recorded on the web or sent into the Patent and Trademark Office. Know that the preparing of your application may take over a year, so this application ought to be documented as quickly as time permits to start the procedure. Status of your application might be checked on the web.

You don't have to hold up until your trademark is broadly enlisted to start ensuring your entitlement to it, be that as it may. When utilizing your business name on showcasing materials or other composed issue, you can exhibit your case to the name as a trademark by including a little "TM" toward the finish of the word. This gives notice to the individuals who see the composed materials that you view the name as exclusive and ought not to be "obtained" by others.

After you get national enlistment of the business name as a trademark, be that as it may, it will get the best conceivable assurance and you may show this by incorporating an R around, "®," toward the finish of your business name.

When you have gotten trademark enrollment, you should record occasional Affidavits of Use with the Patent and Trademark Office to demonstrate that the name stays being used. On the off chance that you stop utilization of the imprint for a time of years, you will lose responsibility for name as a trademark and others might almost certainly use it.

Next comes the matter of "policing" your trademark. This includes online research and examination inside your own industry to decide if your trademarked business name is being utilized by others in the equivalent or comparable business that may cause client disarray as to your business personality.

In that occasion, a wise letter regularly discourages the newcomer from utilizing the business name. In the event that a letter is ineffectual, the issue might be settled through suit.

The establishing of another business is a bustling time, yet it is important to start as fast as conceivable to secure the new business name against encroachment. Along these lines, it is conceivable to counteract client perplexity and hold the majority of the client great will that they have come to connect with your organization's name.

There are few images as recognizable throughout the world as the Coca-Cola brand. Travel to the furthest reaches of the globe and you will probably encounter it on a clock or a sign, if not on the drink itself. Marketers today look to the Coca-Cola brand as a model of marketing power. Its image has transcended national borders and cultural barriers to reach almost everyone on earth. How did the Coca-Cola symbol become such an omnipresent image?

Beginning in 1886, Coca-Cola president John Pemberton began traveling the country introducing pharmacists to the drink. At that time it was considered a medicinal substance that could relieve headaches and other minor woes. Candler distributed clocks, calendars and other items laden with the Coca-Cola logo as he toured the country, spreading the brand and selling his product.

From there the brand continued to penetrate further around the world. The bottling rights to Coca-Cola were sold in 1899 and in 1915 the Root family submitted a standard size bottle for distribution, but it was too fat in the middle. The Coca-Cola Company liked the bottle so much they thinned it down and has been used ever since and is called a Hobbleskirt Bottle. By 1920, with new bottlers springing up all the time, the brand had expanded into Cuba, France, Puerto Rico and other territories. Its world dominance would increase further with World War II, when Coca-Cola promised that "every man in uniform gets a bottle of Coca-Cola for 5 cents, wherever he is, and whatever it costs the company.

" Suddenly Coca-Cola could be found throughout Europe as American GIs carried it with them, and by 1960 the number of countries with Coke bottling plants had doubled.

3.Coca-Cola: The Power of a Brand

Today Coke remains a powerful brand with over a century of history behind it. As a result, items featuring previous incarnations of the Coke image have become classic pieces of Americana. The success of the Coca-Cola brand has made it an icon not just in the world of brand marketing but of American history. It symbolizes the popularity of a soft drink as well as the dominance of American entrepreneurialism in the twentieth century and beyond.

4.MSN just fails to keep it Straight.

Now and then you see advancements go along and you wonder: did they simply do that? The flow of MSN advancement called msnsearchandwin is a prime case of this.

In addition to the fact that they use "dark cap" or possibly "faulty" strategies on the site, yet the informing is conflicting.

In this article, I take a gander at the new MSN advancement and make the inquiry: Why trouble?

At this point, you've most likely caught wind of the new MSN advancement where you can win prizes just by utilizing MSN seek.

They did something directly by enrolling an area name that infers that message. On the off chance that you go to msnsearchandwin.com you will see the natural MSN seek box.

Hold up a minute...Why is this pursuit box blue? Didn't MSN only rebrand with a more pleasant, cleaner silver-dim look?

That, my companions, is botch number one. Maybe the specialized group and the showcasing group didn't inspire together to talk about this program.

That is to say, when you experience something as intricate and gigantic as a rebranding, you should ensure the informing is reliable over the different media. Particularly when the advancement and the rebranding dispatch inside days of one another.

This is shockingly like the article I expounded on Superbowl Ads. In that article, I discussed how sponsors burn through millions on a 30 second or 1 minute TV ad yet they neglect to convey that informing over onto their site adequately if by any stretch of the imagination.

What's more, here we have MSN - likely a standout amongst the most perceived brands on the web and auxiliary to the organization with a standout amongst the best and merciless promoting arms on the planet - and it can't impart its message that MSN is rebranding.

That is to say, how hard would it have been for somebody in Tech to telephone up somebody in Marketing and state, "Coincidentally, you realize that hunt and win advancement you are doing? Make sure that the hues coordinate the new look of MSN that is propelling in a couple of days."

In any case, pause, it shows signs of improvement.

First spotted by Kerry Dean, on the off chance that you see the wellspring of the msnsearchandwin landing page what do you see?

The truth is out, around a million watchwords stuffed into the catchphrases tag. (Alright perhaps not a million but rather there are 256 watchwords in the meta catchphrases tag).

It deteriorates. Promptly beneath the overstuffed watchwords label, you will see a group of catchphrases stuffed into a remarks tag. Again the equivalent 256 words utilized in the meta watchwords tag.

So let me know, is it OK for a web index to spam itself?

Maybe we could all take in a touch of something from MSN's advertising botch: Keep it Consistent!

5.Corporate Branding: Will they remember you?

In the present market offering amount is by all accounts the standard of the day. Slap together something snappy and don't stress over what flies out the entryway, it doesn't make a difference who the buyers are.

Organizations who center around marking will emerge among the group. Why? They have perceived that most purchasers' particularly online purchasers need trust in working with a setup element. Nothing demonstrates your responsibility to your systematic an all around created marking technique.

Having an incredible logo is the primary significant advance toward developing this improvement. Beyond any doubt there are a lot of "out-of-the-case" logo arrangements and the costs are more than speaking to a business that doesn't perceive the estimation of their corporate picture.

The Difference

For what reason would it be advisable for you to spend more than $300 on a logo? OK purchase a vehicle for $1000? Odds are on the off chance that you do you'll pay much more for support and the cerebral pains it will bring. You generally get what you pay for. This can't be focused on enough. On the off chance that you are happy to undermine your business from the earliest starting point by disregarding the picture you depict to your potential customers, that logo will cost you much more than you're willing to contribute.

An expert Graphic Designer will contribute a ton of time, exploring to deliver a logo that is really one of a kind (crucial to marking and making your imprint) and acquaint you with a strong initial phase in Branding your organization as an incredible substance. A logo is additionally upgraded by the components worked around it. With everything identified with plan, everything ought to be uniquely crafted, presently more so than any time in recent memory in light of the fact that the challenge for capital is expanding. You must be superior to your rivals from various perspectives conceivable.

For the youthful new business, spending plans may prohibit you the alternative of working with an expert originator. There are a lot of extraordinary planners out there that won't gouge your wallet yet be sure that they are fit for making precisely what you need and that they have the experience to develop the logo configuration given. You need somebody who is business sharp and has exhibited their connected information.

They should almost certainly anticipate the master plan. The accomplishment of your business lays on this.

Assembling it

As a rule, the more encountered the planner the higher the rates charged. With the experience, you will typically get an item that has been created and refined after some time. A veteran Graphic Designer will plan in light of the comprehensive view taking your speculation dollars further. The numbers cited are with respect to what they produce, a customer will be cheerful to contribute cash when they see return. In the event that the picture created for them pulls in clients, cost ends up auxiliary. Perceive the estimation of your picture and pay attention to your logo very. As individuals we are visual.

For the whole deal

For the most part, a business that has quality administrations to offer and pays attention to their picture will comprehend the benefit of putting resources into an expert structure. Best organizations realize the amount they should give to showcasing so as to produce the business they want. Those advertising dollars will be increasingly viable if your Branding approach was developed legitimately. On the off chance that you take your business truly risks are you'll draw in the equivalent. How would you like to be seen?

A Bit about the Logo

Generally, the center was put around the business mindset as opposed to the logo itself. There are diverse kinds of logos. Numerous vast companies use entirely content or shortenings. Organizations like DELL, IBM, RCA, ABB, and so on. Content logos are exceptionally well known and are effectively coordinated over the Branding board.

Notorious medications are likewise used by numerous organizations. A symbol can be exceptionally incredible in recognizing an organization. Take Apple or Nike for instance. Utilizing symbolism is an extremely incredible technique in marking. Images manage us in our lives and everyday exercises. Symbols can be extremely basic and clean to progressively complex using angles and reproduced 3D. Illustrative (past famous) is less much of the time utilized yet can work successfully for organizations that generally need to depict immortality or "regular" comfortable inclination commonly found on a jug of tomato sauce or natural potato chips.

Everything illustrated above can direct the cost of your logo. The logo is an amazing part of your organization. It should require investment to make and will require much consideration on the off chance that it is to make a ground-breaking Branding procedure.

Make sure that the logo originator of decision is happy to furnish you with mockups and different amendments and is eager to help take your organization to the following dimension.

6.Good to mention.

A decent logo configuration is exceedingly instrumental in building up a business brand and making a dependable impression among its clients. It ought to almost certainly make an amazing effect on the watchers and effectively radiate the nature and frame of mind of a business. In a perfect world, an organization logo configuration ought to almost certainly impart your organization ethos, standards, mission and the idea of item/administration offered, to the watchers.

An expert logo configuration would build up an expert picture of your organization and reinforce your image. As a matter of fact, much of the time, the purchaser gets the early introduction of the organization through your logo.

Your business logo should fabricate a brand that is sufficiently able to give your buyer a visual symbolism of your organization. Individuals ought to most likely distinguish your organization without hesitation of your logo.

The pattern appears, a large portion of the great logos are straightforward and frequently message based. Think about the IBM, SONY or Microsoft logo, regardless of whether you see a piece of it you will probably perceive the organization. It is incredibly basic for a logo to be simple for individuals to recall.

This standard of effortlessness applies in most cases, be that as it may, we regularly observe exemptions in Government Organizations, Hotels, and Luxury resorts and so on in light of the fact that they need to set up an established selective picture. This again conveys us to a vital point that ought to be considered for a decent logo structure - the nature of business.

While effortlessness can be the fundamental rule for any logo plan, the structures may shift broadly relying upon the idea of business. For instance, a monetary foundation may get a kick out of the chance to utilize a boldface text style to express solidarity and stableness though a messenger administration or transport organization may lean toward emphasized textual styles to express the speed and development engaged with their business.

Furthermore, while indicating the plan prerequisites for your logo you ought to consider the way that you will most likely need to utilize your logo on your fax spread and different spots where it will be in highly contrasting. You ought to guarantee that your logo looks similarly great and alluring in high contrast.

I would likewise propose staying away from a stylish search for your logo on the off chance that you are making arrangements for a long haul business since what we concern "present day" today may be predated tomorrow. It is essential that your logo creator realizes how to keep up this equalization.

While any expert logo architect ought to probably make a custom logo plan once you have furnished them with your details, you ought to be mindful so as to choose an accomplished structuring organization and not arrive up with some single planner start-up endeavor.

Last yet not the least critical factor is cost. You are paying for your logo - something that will be utilized to set up your image and speak to your business for quite a long time, so you ought to be prepared to pay a good sum while it is additionally not important to pay some enormous sum like $350 for a logo.

With the online logo configuration firms coming into business, presently you have a wide decision of cost for your logos and it ought not to be hard to discover a logo planner that accommodates your financial plan. Some logo configuration locales would even enable you to cite your own cost for your logo.

In the event that you have still not got a logo for your business or are not content with your current logo, it's time you get your new logo. Wish you lucked with your logo chase.

www.ingramcontent.com/pod-product-compliance
Lightning Source LLC
Chambersburg PA
CBHW072206170526
45158CB00004BB/1784